ALCOHOL AND DRUG OFFENSES

YOUR LEGAL RIGHTS

CORONA BREZINA

ROSEN
PUBLISHING

New York

Published in 2015 by The Rosen Publishing Group, Inc.
29 East 21st Street, New York, NY 10010

Expert Reviewer: Lindsay A. Lewis, Esq.

Library of Congress Cataloging-in-Publication Data

Brezina, Corona, author.
Alcohol and drug offenses : your legal rights/Corona Brezina.
    pages cm.—(Know your rights)
Includes bibliographical references and index.
ISBN 978-1-4777-8032-9 (library bound) — ISBN 978-1-4777-8033-6
(pbk.) — ISBN 978-1-4777-8034-3 (6-pack)
1. Narcotic laws—Juvenile literature. 2. Drugs of abuse—Law and
legislation—Criminal provisions—Juvenile literature. I. Title.
K3641.B74 2015
345.73'0277—dc23

2014021740

Manufactured in the United States of America

CONTENTS

DeMarcus Sanders was attending college and working at a janitorial job when he was arrested on a first-time charge for possession of marijuana in Waterloo, Iowa. He was sentenced to thirty days in jail and a fine, but Sanders was unable to get his life back on track after being freed. He lost his job and college credits. His driver's license was suspended, and the state refused to reinstate it since he was unable to pay thousands of dollars in fines. Waterloo is a small city without much public transportation. Sanders had trouble finding a job that didn't require driving to work. Without steady work, he couldn't earn money to pay the fines.

Sanders's case serves as one example of the consequences of a drug conviction in the United States. If Sanders were arrested today in California on a first-time possession charge, he would probably receive only the equivalent of a ticket, requiring that he pay a small fine. If he lived in Colorado, possessing marijuana would be legal. In some other states, however, he might face an even harsher sentence than Iowa's penalties. As in this case, even a first-time possession can have consequences. A college student could lose financial aid or become ineligible for a job in an FDIC-regulated organization such as a bank or in law enforcement. Whatever the charge, in whichever state it happens, it is best to talk to a lawyer to get the best possible outcome.

Sanders's case demonstrates another trend in the enforcement of drug laws. According to analysis by the American Civil Liberties Union (ACLU), an African American person is more than three times as likely to be arrested for marijuana possession as a white person, even

A 2013 ACLU report found racial disparities in marijuana possession arrests across the United States. These disparities increased between 2001 and 2010.

though both groups use marijuana at about the same rates. In the ACLU report, Sanders describes how he felt targeted because of his race. On a later occasion, police detained and searched him after he crossed a street in downtown Waterloo, even though he had not violated any laws. They found marijuana in his possession and issued a citation. Sanders fought the case, claiming that his constitutional rights had been violated. A judge agreed, ruling in his favor.

Anyone involved in a court case will benefit from knowing his or her legal rights and understanding how to navigate the system. The justice and penal system can be bewilderingly complex. A young person suddenly thrown into this system often lacks the basic legal information that could help achieve the best possible outcome. Drug-related crimes often involve serious charges punishable by severe penalties. Even petty charges can have lifelong repercussions if not handled correctly. It is important to take any and all cases seriously.

Everybody can benefit from having legal savvy, regardless of personal involvement in the system. Understanding the consequences up front, and knowing what kind of action to take in the event of a summons or arrest, can lessen negative consequences. If you possess some fundamental knowledge about federal, state, and local laws and the typical penalties for various crimes, you can share this information with family and friends. More importantly, you can learn how to avoid getting into trouble with the law.

CHAPTER 1

ALCOHOL

A lcoholism is a public health problem in the United States. The National Institute on Alcohol Abuse and Alcoholism lists alcohol-related causes as the third leading preventable cause of death in the United States. It costs nearly eighty-five thousand people their lives every year. Nearly a quarter of all Americans reported in a 2012 survey that they had engaged in binge drinking in the previous month, and 7.1 percent qualified as heavy drinkers. However, fewer than one out of five people with alcohol abuse disorders sought treatment. Alcohol problems cost the nation about $224 billion annually in lost productivity, health care, and property damage costs.

About one out of five teenagers reported riding in a car driven by someone who had been drinking alcohol, and one out of ten teens reported that they drove after drinking.

Alcohol use is also an issue for teenagers. According to the annual Monitoring the Future survey, which tracks substance use among young adults, more teenagers abuse alcohol than any other substance. About seven out of ten teens have used alcohol before finishing high school, and three out of ten eighth-graders have used alcohol. Over half of all high school seniors and one out of eight eighth-graders have been drunk. However, overall rates of alcohol use by teens have been declining since 2002.

THE LEGAL DRINKING AGE

Most people know that twenty-one is the legal drinking age in the United States, and that it's illegal for anyone younger to consume alcohol. However, there are varying laws and policies about alcohol possession that are subject to federal, state, and local control. Adults younger than twenty-one are generally prohibited from possessing alcohol, but certain limited exceptions are regulated by state laws.

Until the 1980s, there was no national minimum drinking age. During the 1960s and 1970s, many states reduced the legal drinking age to eighteen, nineteen, or twenty years. Concern grew during the early 1980s about the higher rate of drunken driving fatalities in states with lower minimum drinking ages. The National Minimum Drinking Age Act of 1984 was passed to address the issue. It set the national minimum drinking age at twenty-one years.

Laws concerning alcohol, however, fall under both federal and state authority. The federal government regu- lates importation and taxation of alcohol. States set their own laws for sales, distribution, possession, and importation of alcohol across state lines. Under the U.S. Constitution, the federal government does not have the authority to impose a condition, such as a minimum drinking age that would interfere with the states' rights to determine their own laws.

The National Minimum Drinking Age Act got around this limitation by requiring states to reset their laws to a minimum drinking age of twenty-one. (In Canada, provinces and territories set their own liquor laws, and the legal drinking age is set at either eighteen or nineteen across the country.) States had the option of refusing, but the decision would be costly; any state that did not raise the minimum drinking age to twenty-one would have its federal funding for highways cut by 10 percent. By 1988, every state had complied with the requirements of the act.

The standards set by the National Minimum Drinking Age Act prohibit anyone under age twenty-one from buying or publicly possessing any alcoholic beverage. Nevertheless, states can permit exceptions concerning possession in instances such as religious purposes

Serving alcohol to minors can have serious consequences for an establishment as well. Security people often check ID at the door.

(generally when accompanied by a parent), legitimate medical purposes, activities on private property, or handling through the course of employment, meaning that a minor can work at a place that sells alcohol. Many states have a family exception, whereby a minor, for example, can drink alcohol legally if his or her parents are present. Some states have a location exception, in which a minor may be allowed to consume alcohol at a private location or private residence, sometimes specified to be a parent's residence. Many states allow minors to purchase alcohol specifically for "law enforcement purposes," in other words, to identify merchants who are willing to break the law by selling alcohol to minors.

States also set their own prohibitions and penalties for youth violations involving alcohol. These address the sale, purchase, possession, and consumption of alcohol by minors. Not every state prohibits all these activities. Some states ban minors from entering drinking establishments, and some prohibit "internal possession" of alcohol that can be proven by a blood or urine test, regardless of whether there is any direct evidence of possession or consumption. An overview of state policies can be viewed at the Alcohol Policy Information System website (see sources at the back of this book). Specific laws can be found at state websites and the sites of Canadian provincial and territorial governments.

UNDER THE INFLUENCE

Alcohol represents a significant factor in contributing to crime. According to a Bureau of Justice analysis, alcohol was involved in at least 20 percent of violent crimes. Unsurprisingly, incidents of alcohol-related violence tended to take place late at night or on weekends, often in the home or at bars.

Several categories of crimes are closely associated with alcohol, most of which involve drinking and driving. According to the Centers for Disease Control and Prevention, nearly a third of all traffic deaths involve an alcohol-impaired driver. Young adults are particularly at risk, since drivers between ages sixteen and twenty are seventeen times more likely to die in an accident when

It's illegal for a driver on the road to have an open container of alcohol within reach, even if the driver isn't drinking.

they have a blood-alcohol concentration of .08 percent—the legal limit—than when they have not been drinking. However, the rates of drunk driving by teens have decreased by more than 50 percent since 1991.

Drunk drivers can be charged with driving under the influence (DUI) or driving while intoxicated (DWI), depending on the terminology of state law. The intoxicant might be alcohol, drugs, or both. DUI/DWI is a very serious charge that carries harsh penalties. A police officer may require a Breathalyzer or blood test to determine the alcohol level or presence of drugs in a person's system. Any blood alcohol level of .08 percent or above qualifies as being under the influence.

Specific charges and penalties for DUI/DWI vary from one state to another. Depending on the circumstances, the charge may be either a felony or misdemeanor. A felony is a serious crime, with a range of punishments varying from imprisonment of more than a year to the death penalty, depending on the severity of the crime. A misdemeanor is a less serious crime with lighter punishment. Both are criminal convictions, as opposed to a violation, which does not come with a conviction or jail time. In the event you are charged with a DUI or DWI, you should immediately consult a lawyer, who will explain the potential consequences of a conviction and might be able to negotiate a more favorable outcome, such as a plea to a violation, or a lesser crime.

In many states, it is a violation of the law to possess an open container of alcohol or to drink in public places, including the street or a beach. If you are caught with an open container containing an alcoholic beverage, you might receive a summons to appear in court. The most common disposition of such a case would be a plea to the violation and a fine. The violation would remain on your record for a short time during which potential employers would be able to see it. You may seek early sealing of your record so that a private employer would not see the violation, but it would still be available to government agencies, even if it is sealed. It is best to consult with a lawyer to be sure the violation would not have negative consequences for you in the future.

Public intoxication—sometimes called drunk and disorderly conduct or disturbing the peace—is considered a crime in many states. Generally, the offender is detained for threatening or disruptive behavior. Public intoxication is usually considered a misdemeanor, and penalties may include imprisonment, a fine, or treatment for alcohol abuse.

Minors can be detained for possessing or consuming alcohol. These are defined as status offenses—conduct that is illegal for a juvenile but noncriminal for an adult. Juvenile offenders caught drinking or possessing alcohol may be referred to juvenile or adult court. Possible penalties may include a fine, community service, participation in an alcohol education program, or suspension of a driver's license.

Public intoxication laws are intended to preserve the safe use and enjoyment of public spaces.

13

MAKING ALCOHOL ILLEGAL: PROHIBITION

Alcohol unquestionably has serious public health consequences that some experts claim are more severe than the combined impact of all illegal drugs. In 2014, President Barack Obama offhandedly compared legal and illegal vices. "As has been well documented, I smoked pot as a kid, and I view it as a bad habit and a vice, not very different from the cigarettes that I smoked as a young person up through a big chunk of my adult life," Obama told writer David Remnick of the *New Yorker*. "I don't think it is more dangerous than alcohol."

If alcohol is harmful to public health, why isn't there more pressure to increase restrictions or ban it? The United States did try a wholesale ban on alcohol—called Prohibition—during the early part of the twentieth century. It was an experiment that ended in disaster.

Prohibition came about through heavy political and social pressure that evolved during the late nineteenth century. Church leaders and community organizations worked diligently to convince politicians and the public as a whole of the evils of alcohol. They often cited crime, poverty, domestic abuse, and poor health as the results of drinking. Congress ultimately listened and passed the Eighteenth Amendment to the U.S. Constitution banning the manufacture, sale, and distribution of alcohol in 1917, and prohibition became the law of the land in January 1920.

Prohibition did not have its intended effect. The amendment did not ban the consumption of alcohol, though the law made it harder to legally purchase it. The demand for illegal alcohol, some of it highly toxic, soared, and networks of illegal production were established throughout the country. The legal system was strained as jails and courtrooms were soon packed with people charged with making, hauling, or selling

Police raid a basement in New York where suspects were producing alcohol using an illegal still.

alcohol. To make matters worse, violent criminal organizations took control of the distribution networks.

After nearly a decade, Congress had to admit that the effort had been a failure. In 1933, the Nineteenth Amendment to the Constitution, which ended Prohibition, became law.

PROBLEMS WITH PURCHASING AND POSSESSING ALCOHOL

In addition to prohibiting consumption and possession of alcohol to minors, states ban the sale of alcohol to and purchase of alcohol by minors. State laws vary on the penalties for a minor trying to buy alcohol; however, they all consider certain alcohol-related activities to be offenses. Attempting to purchase alcohol is in itself an offense. Making false statements while attempting to purchase alcohol—such as claiming to be twenty-one years old—might also qualify in some states as yet another offense. Trying to buy alcohol with a false ID or using someone else's ID can result in a potentially more serious charge. Possessing a false ID might be a minor misdemeanor or something more serious, like a felony.

The consequences of alcohol possession and consumption by minors can go beyond the underage drinkers themselves. An adult who lends an ID to a minor or provides a minor with a false ID can also be charged with an offense. In many states, it is illegal for adults to supply minors with alcohol. The penalties for violations can be severe, especially if it is a second offense or if the minor causes serious injury while under the influence of alcohol. In addition, merchants who sell alcohol to minors risk losing their liquor license. In some states, the seller is liable even if he or she took all possible steps to avoid knowingly selling alcohol to a minor.

CHAPTER 2

MARIJUANA

Marijuana is the most commonly used illicit drug in the United States. Marijuana use is also becoming increasingly accepted in society. In a 2014 survey by the Pew Research Center, a nonpartisan fact tank, 54 percent of participants reported that they favored legalizing marijuana. The results marked a drastic increase from 1969—the first year the survey was taken—when just 12 percent favored legalization. Public support has grown quickly and sharply, with support rising 13 percentage points since 2010. Support is highest among younger Americans who were born after 1980.

Marijuana has a long history of cultivation and use in the United States. The Pilgrims brought the crop with them from England in the seventeenth century, and George Washington and Thomas Jefferson both grew thousands of acres of hemp—the cannabis plant that produces marijuana. They produced it primarily for products

In the seventeenth century, hemp fiber was in such high demand that some American colonies required farmers to grow the crop.

such as cloth, rope, and paper, but it was also used medicinally.

Until the early twentieth century, few laws restricted drug use or sales in the United States. Patent medicines commonly contained many substances that are now illegal, including cannabis extracts. The first federal law regulating drugs, passed in 1906, required that ingredients be listed on patented medicines. Marijuana was not federally regulated until 1937, when the Marihuana Tax Act effectively made it illegal. In 1970, the Controlled Substances Act—part of the Comprehensive Drug Abuse Prevention and Control Act—classified marijuana as a Schedule I drug, meaning that it was considered to have a very high potential for abuse and no accepted medical use.

In 2014, nearly half of all Americans had tried marijuana. According to the Monitoring the Future survey, marijuana use has increased since 2007 while use of other drugs has remained steady. In a 2013 survey, 7 percent of eighth-graders, 18 percent of tenth-graders, and 22.7 percent of twelfth-graders reported using marijuana the month before, marking an increase in every age group over 2008 survey results. Use of marijuana is highest among young adults in their late teens and twenties, according to the National Institute on Drug Abuse.

MARIJUANA POSSESSION AND USE

Federal law does not reflect the increasing public acceptance of marijuana. Some groups, including the American Medical Association, have urged the federal government to review marijuana's Schedule I classification to promote clinical research on using it to treat various conditions. Certain compounds isolated from marijuana, however, have been approved for medical use by the FDA.

Under federal law, it is illegal to grow, sell, or possess marijuana or to sell marijuana paraphernalia. Growing or selling marijuana qualifies as felony drug trafficking. The penalty is determined by the weight or number of plants. (For other substances, weight is the only measurement.) The mandatory minimum penalty for someone caught with one

A Seattle resident takes marijuana out of a plastic bag. Washington's legalization of marijuana for recreational use conflicts with federal law.

thousand plants or one thousand kilograms of marijuana is ten years to life in prison, as well as a fine. The penalty for a misdemeanor possession of marijuana is up to a year in prison, as well as a fine. Penalties increase for repeat offenders. For example, a repeat offender can have a sentence start at twenty years imprisonment. If the drug causes serious bodily injury or death, the minimum sentence is also twenty years.

In August 2013, Attorney General Eric Holder issued a memorandum to federal prosecutors refining federal charging policy regarding mandatory minimum sentences for certain nonviolent, low-level drug offenders. This new policy, in theory, would make federal sentencing for drug offenses somewhat less strict for first-time and low-level offenders. In early 2014, Holder called for reduced sentences generally for low-level drug users.

The Department of Justice issues guidelines that emphasize priorities in enforcing the law. Pursuing minor offenders using medical marijuana, for example, would be an inefficient use of federal money. In 2013, the Department of Justice set forth its priorities in a memo regarding laws related to marijuana:

- Preventing the distribution of marijuana to minors
- Preventing revenue from the sale of marijuana from going to criminal enterprises, gangs, and cartels
- Preventing the diversion of marijuana from states where it is legal under state law in some form to other states

- Preventing state-authorized marijuana activity from being used as a cover or pretext for the trafficking of other illegal drugs or other illegal activity
- Preventing violence and the use of firearms in the cultivation and distribution of marijuana
- Preventing drugged driving and the exacerbation of other adverse public health consequences associated with marijuana use
- Preventing the growing of marijuana on public lands and the attendant public safety and environmental dangers posed by marijuana production on public lands
- Preventing marijuana possession or use on federal property

The guidelines did not diminish federal authority to prosecute marijuana crimes at every level. They merely provided recommendations on using discretion in investigating and prosecuting violations of the law.

Federal law concerning marijuana crimes supersedes state and local laws. Therefore, in cities and states where laws and penalties for marijuana crimes have been relaxed, users could still legally be charged with a federal crime carrying a much harsher sentence.

MEDICINAL MARIJUANA

In 1996, California became the first state to legalize medical marijuana. Supporters of medical marijuana gathered signatures to bring the issue directly to the voters on the ballot. Proposition 215, legalizing medical marijuana in California, passed with 56 percent of the vote.

Since then, supporters of medical marijuana across the country have followed the example set in California by introducing the measure on state ballots. Twenty states

In 1994 and 1995, California legislators attempted to introduce state laws legalizing medical marijuana, but the governor vetoed the measure despite popular support.

and the District of Columbia now allow the medical use of marijuana.

The laws regulating medical marijuana exist as a patchwork that varies from one state to another. Patients typically have to register with the state to qualify for medical use of marijuana. This can exempt them from being arrested for some drug charges. Medical conditions that qualify patients for medical marijuana use also vary greatly from one state to another. California, for example, allows for medical marijuana use to treat a wide variety of conditions, while New Mexico permits only patients with very specific conditions to qualify. Regulations often detail how many plants patients or medical marijuana growers can cultivate. Medical marijuana dispensaries themselves are subject to rules. Local laws might also affect medical marijuana sales and use. For example, some municipalities have banned marijuana dispensaries within city limits. Many states have only recently legalized marijuana and are still in the process of determining implementation and restrictions.

Legalization of medical marijuana complicates the cooperation between state and federal law enforcement agencies in enforcing the law. The 2013 Department of Justice memo made clear the expectation that states would establish "strong and effective regulatory and enforcement systems" to keep marijuana-related activities from contributing to crime and public health problems. If state agencies fail to keep order, federal agencies might take action.

BAD DRUGS, GOOD MEDICINE

The Controlled Substances Act of 1970 put an end to research on the Schedule I drugs deemed to have no legitimate medical use. Nonetheless, some doctors and scientists consider certain hallucinogenic drugs to have potential in treating mental illness. In the late 2000s, researchers began proposing new research trials involving hallucinogens. In 2009, the FDA approved a Harvard clinical trial evaluating whether LSD could relieve anxiety in cancer patients. A study at Johns Hopkins examined whether psilocybin—the active chemical agent in "magic mushrooms"—could help treat chronic addiction. Several studies have shown that hallucinogens could help people with conditions such as depression, anxiety, obsessive-compulsive disorder, and severe cluster headaches. The anesthetic drug ketamine has also shown potential for treating depression, and Ecstasy has shown promise in treating post-traumatic stress disorder (PTSD), which can severely affect the daily lives of sufferers.

Positive clinical results do not mean that hallucinogens will be approved for medical use any time soon. Much more research would be needed to evaluate the safety of the drugs and their appropriate use.

THE LEGALIZE MARIJUANA MOVEMENT

In 2012, voters in Colorado and Washington approved the legalization of marijuana for recreational use. For adults twenty-one and older, use and possession of small amounts of marijuana would no longer be a crime. Voters in Colorado approved legalization of marijuana by passing an amendment to the state constitution. Colorado began legal sales of marijuana in January 2014. Voters in Washington State approved a ballot initiative with a plan to allow the first licensed sellers to open in mid-2014. Debate over the pros and cons of legalizing marijuana continues across the nation, with supporters of legalization working to put ballot measures before voters. The next states likely to put it to a vote include Alaska, Oregon, California, and Arizona. Voters in a few cities, including Portland, Maine, have also approved measures legalizing marijuana for recreational use.

In Colorado, marijuana is regulated very much like alcohol. Marijuana use is prohibited in public. Driving under the influence of marijuana is illegal, as is selling

A customer examines marijuana choices in Denver on January 1, 2014, the first day of legalized recreational marijuana sales in the state of Colorado.

marijuana to minors. But there are a few differences. Marijuana cannot be taken across state lines. Retailers can sell only marijuana farmed by licensed Colorado growers. Colorado's new "adult-use" system coordinates with the existing regulations and controls for sales of medical marijuana.

Recreational marijuana is heavily taxed in Colorado, which brings in new revenue for the state. It could potentially save money by eliminating the costs of prosecuting minor marijuana possession. Opponents of legalization argue that the consequences of marijuana use and abuse could represent a public health cost.

The regulation and enforcement of marijuana use is being left at the state level for now. The federal government included consideration of recreational marijuana in its 2013 memo on enforcement priorities. As Colorado prepared to allow legal sales of marijuana, state officials kept Department of Justice officials closely updated on their plans to regulate use and enforce the new law. Colorado represents a test case for marijuana legalization. The federal government will not intervene as long as the state system continues to work.

MARIJUANA AND CRIME

While some states have legalized marijuana for medicinal and even recreational purposes, the consequences for marijuana possession in other states can vary greatly. In some places, marijuana possession is a minor, ticketable offense, like a traffic violation. In others, police have the option of issuing a ticket or arresting the offender. And in many states, marijuana possession is a misdemeanor crime, with penalties varying depending on state law. In Louisiana, for example, a first-time possession charge of a small amount of marijuana can result in six months imprisonment along with a fine.

Sixteen states have decriminalized marijuana. However, decriminalization is not the same as legalization. It means that first-time offenders are not charged with a crime for possessing a small amount of marijuana. Instead, they are issued a ticket. Adults do not have the incident put on their criminal record. First-time juvenile offenders may avoid being referred to the juvenile justice system. After California decriminalized marijuana in 2010, the state saw a 20 percent drop in arrests of juvenile offenders in 2011, bringing juvenile crime rate to the lowest level in state history. Most of the change was due to the 61 percent decline in arrests for marijuana possession.

In addition to states, some cities and counties have passed laws decriminalizing marijuana. Supporters of decriminalization claim that it saves money for states by cutting costs to the criminal justice system. For example, it keeps many young small-time offenders out of the juvenile justice system.

Opponents argue that decriminalization leads to addiction and other social ills, and that it sends the wrong message to adolescents. In some states, like New York, those charged with a violation for possession of marijuana might be eligible upon the motion of the defendant (or his or her lawyer) to have the action adjourned in contemplation of dismissal (also called an ACD). This would result in a dismissal after a period of six months if the person charged was not involved in any other illegal activity and had no further arrests or summons. This option is available only for those without prior ACDs for marijuana possession and who have generally clean records. It suggests a more lenient treatment of personal-use marijuana possession under the law.

Even as some states relax penalties for marijuana crimes, others continue to strictly enforce existing laws. According to Federal Bureau of Investigation (FBI) statistics, in 2012, about 750,000 people in the United States were arrested for crimes involving marijuana. More than 658,000 of those arrests were for marijuana possession alone. Many states still impose mandatory minimum sentences on some marijuana crimes, especially for repeat offenders and offenses involving sales or trafficking.

According to a 2013 ACLU report, arrests for marijuana crimes show a trend of racial bias. The analysis showed that whites and African Americans were about equally likely to use marijuana, but African Americans were nearly four times as likely to be arrested for marijuana possession. In addition, the racial disparity has increased—while the arrest rate for whites remained steady at about 192 arrests per 100,000, the arrest rate for African Americans increased from 537 per 100,000 in 2001 to 716 per in 2010. The report also showed that 62 percent of arrests were of offenders under age twenty-four, with 34 percent of offenders being teenagers or younger.

CHAPTER 3

ILLEGAL AND ILLICIT DRUGS

J ohn Coffey Jr. started using drugs as a way to deal with his grief following his father's sudden death from a heart attack. He was nineteen years old at the time and had recently turned down a chance to play baseball for a local community college in Michigan. Instead of finding a positive way to deal with his grief, the former star pitcher began abusing prescription drugs. A friend recommended that he try the painkiller OxyContin, and after two weeks of swallowing and snorting the pills, he was hooked.

The pills became expensive and hard to get, but Coffey was addicted. Heroin offered the same high but was cheaper and easier to buy. By age twenty-four, he was taking the drug to hold back his withdrawal symptoms. Heroin

Prescription drug abuse can lead to dangerous side effects, overdose, harmful drug interactions, and addiction.

became the most important thing in his life. He hated the drug but couldn't stop using it, even after a close friend from his high school died from an overdose. He lost several jobs due to his addiction and began committing crimes to pay for it. In 2009, he and his half brother—also an addict— were arrested after allegedly breaking into several homes and stealing more than $24,000 in jewelry, electronics, and other items that they intended to sell. John Coffey was sentenced to eight to twenty years in prison.

Today, Coffey is focused on telling his story to make drugs less appealing. During a 2011 interview with MLive reporter Danielle Salisbury, he admitted, "That drug had such a hold on me, I lost everything."

Stories like Coffey's are taking place across the country. In 2014, nearly 90 percent of all Americans considered drug abuse either a crisis or a serious problem, according to the Pew Research Center. Public support of the decriminalization and legalization of marijuana has not extended to other illicit drugs. (An illicit drug might be a substance that is legal but sold without a prescription and used for recreation.) But the report shows that many people have been reconsidering their attitudes on the consequences for drug users. More have begun to view drug abuse and addiction as a public health issue that should be treated rather than a crime that should be punished. Two-thirds of people surveyed approved of states abandoning mandatory minimum sentences for nonviolent drug offenders.

According to the 2013 Monitoring the Future survey, use of most illegal and illicit drugs other than marijuana remained relatively stable from previous recent years.

Nonmedical use of prescription drugs continued to represent a significant problem, but the rate of use did not change much. Use of synthetic marijuana, inhalants, cocaine, and Vicodin declined slightly; use of a synthetic drug known as bath salts increased slightly.

ILLEGAL DRUGS

The legal framework that regulates illegal drugs today was set up in 1970, with the passage of the Comprehensive Drug Abuse Prevention and Control Act. Before it was passed, a hodgepodge of different laws was applied to crimes involving individual drugs. The act addressed all drugs of abuse, including illegal drugs as well as drugs with legitimate medical use.

The act categorized drugs of abuse into five levels of control. As previously mentioned, Schedule I drugs have a very high potential for abuse and no accepted medical use. Schedule II drugs also are considered to have a very high potential for abuse, but they have some accepted medical use which is very strictly regulated. Because of their effects on health and behavior, these drugs are considered to be a danger to the user, to others, and to society. There are nearly two hundred illegal drugs listed on Schedule I and II, but most are unfamiliar and not widely available.

Illegal drugs are classified into four categories: opiates/opioids—also called narcotics—hallucinogens, stimulants, and depressants. Some common Schedule I drugs include heroin (an opiate), LSD (a hallucinogen), and Ecstasy (a stimulant). Common Schedule II drugs include the opioids methadone, oxycodone (sold as the brand

A recovering addict takes a dose of methadone, a drug used to treat heroin addiction. Like many teenage drug abusers, he started out with prescription painkillers.

names OxyContin and Percocet), and fentanyl; the opiates opium, morphine, and codeine; and the stimulants cocaine, amphetamine, methamphetamine, and methylphenidate (sold as Ritalin).

Drugs in Schedules III, IV, and V have accepted medical use and varying abuse potential. Schedule III and IV drugs have a high or moderate potential for abuse and are available with a doctor's prescription. Schedule V drugs have a low potential for abuse and are generally available without a prescription.

Federal agencies such as the Drug Enforcement Agency (DEA) focus efforts on stopping drug traffickers. Penalties for an individual trafficking large quantities of some of the most common Schedule I and Schedule II drugs range from five years and a $5 million fine to a life sentence for more massive amounts. Penalties are greater for repeat offenders. For individual trafficking of more obscure drugs in all categories, federal penalties are less severe.

Most drug possession cases are prosecuted under state laws. States can set their own penalties for the sale, manufacture, distribution, cultivation, possession, or use of illegal and illicit drugs. Drug possession of small amounts of a substance is either considered a misdemeanor offense or a felony, depending on the drug. Possession of a larger amount automatically can be considered possession with the intent to distribute—based on the sheer volume of the drugs possessed—which carries harsher penalties.

Certain other factors might also result in a stiffer penalty. Some states impose mandatory minimum sentences for certain drug convictions, meaning that a judge can't give an offender a lighter sentence based on the circumstances. For example, under Idaho law, anyone caught holding more than 28 grams of cocaine or methamphetamine is sentenced to a mandatory minimum prison term of three years along with a fine of $10,000. Repeat offenders are likely to receive harsher penalties. Being caught with drugs near a school or certain public buildings, or in the presence of a minor, may require an increased sentence. Someone who associates with another person holding drugs can also be charged with possession, regardless of whether he or she even had contact with the drug.

States also have laws dealing with drug trafficking, defined as manufacturing, distributing, dispensing, or possessing with intent to manufacture, distribute, or dispense a controlled substance. It is also a crime to conspire with others to deal drugs, and you can be charged with a drug dealing or trafficking conspiracy even if you never possess or sell the drugs. If you lend your car so that someone can transport drugs or drive a person somewhere to sell drugs, it could be a liability to you. Penalties for dealing drugs are much harsher than for simple possession. They might carry a sentence of five years in prison and a fine. Dealing drugs can result in harsh penalties under federal law, anywhere from probation up to life in prison, depending on the amount of drugs involved and sold and the specific circumstances of the offense.

Specific laws and penalties vary greatly from one state to another, and the laws are frequently revised. However, the trend in both state and federal court is toward rehabilitation. There are many drug treatment programs available to offenders. These can be offered as alternatives to jail. A convicted offender can stay out of prison as long as he or she abides by the terms of the program. Rehabilitation might also be offered in exchange for a shorter sentence. One such program is the Residential Drug Abuse Program (RDAP) offered at certain federal institutions for qualifying offenders. Upon completion, participation often results in quicker placement in a halfway house and a reduced sentence. There are restrictions to these programs: violent offenders might be ineligible, and it is subject to available space. However, the program offers the advantage of providing treatment, as well as a bargaining chip in plea negotiations to get a defendant a more lenient sentence.

THE WAR ON DRUGS

For most of the twentieth century, drug laws gradually became more and more restrictive. Drugs such as opium, cocaine, heroin, and marijuana were gradually outlawed during the first few decades of the century. During the 1960s, drug use came to be viewed as a serious societal problem, leading to further restrictions that culminated in the 1970 Comprehensive Drug Abuse Prevention and Control Act. In the 1970s, President Richard Nixon created the DEA. Rates of arrests for drug offenses increased. In the 1980s, as crack cocaine became a serious public concern, President Ronald Reagan waged a war on drugs, ushering in harsher penalties and longer sentences, mainly for crack-cocaine convictions. The numbers of people imprisoned for drug-related crimes increased sharply, and the United States came to have the highest rates of imprisonment for drug crimes of any country in the world. Few politicians protested antidrug efforts since they did not want to be viewed as soft on the issue of drugs or crime.

In 2012, of about 12.2 million arrests made nationwide, the greatest number was for drug-related crimes, at about 1.6 million arrests, according to the FBI. Most of these arrests—82.2 percent—were for drug possession, with 42.4 percent for marijuana possession. The remaining 17.8 percent of drug-related arrests were for crimes related

THE PROBLEM WITH PRESCRIPTIONS

In 2013, the DEA released a report that described abuse of controlled prescription drugs as the fastest-growing drug problem in the United States. Prescription drugs were the second most commonly abused category of drugs, behind marijuana. Opioid painkillers were the most common cause of drug overdoses. Prescription drug abuse has also contributed to an increase in heroin use, as some users eventually find that heroin is cheaper or more easily obtained than prescription drugs. A recent study published in the *Journal of the American Medical Association* (JAMA), found that heroin users are increasingly white, suburban, and young.

According to the 2011 National Survey on Drug Use and Health, 6.1 million people—or 2.1 percent of the population—used prescription drugs illicitly. The most commonly abused type of drug was painkillers, used by 4.5 million people. Other categories included pain relievers, stimulants, and sedatives. The 2013 Monitoring the Future survey of teenagers found that out of the fourteen most-abused categories of drugs, seven were pharmaceutical. These included Adderall, Vicodin, cough medicine, tranquilizers, sedatives, OxyContin, and Ritalin.

Many people trying drugs for the first time begin with nonmedical use of prescription drugs in the mistaken belief that they're safer than illegal drugs. Most users get prescription drugs from friends and relatives, often diverting them from a legitimate prescription for recreational use. Some abusers also obtain prescription drugs through forged prescriptions or from "pill mills," clinics that make such drugs easily available.

Federal and state agencies have responded to the prescription drug problem with education and enforcement efforts. Educational measures aim to make the public and health care providers more aware of the abuse potential of

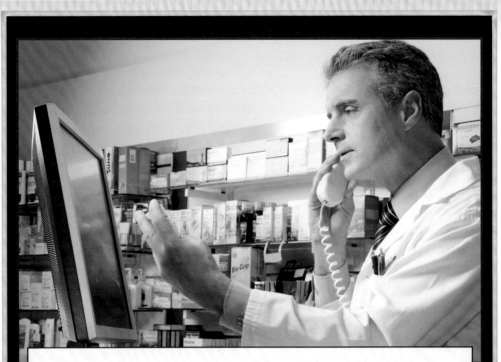

A pharmacist checks that a prescription is valid. Prescription drug monitoring programs can help prevent drugs from being diverted for illegitimate purposes.

prescription drugs. Tracking and monitoring programs aim to prevent prescription drugs from being diverted for nonmedical use. Law enforcement actions target pill mills and prescription drug traffickers. Improved access to substance abuse treatment programs could help users struggling with prescription drug addiction.

Some prescription drug addicts eventually switch to using heroin, a drug with an effect similar to that of many opioid painkillers. According to the Substance Abuse and Mental Health Services Administration, 81 percent of heroin users began by abusing prescription drugs. Users who turn to heroin as a substitute for opioid painkillers are more likely to overdose, since the dosage and purity of heroin is impossible to determine.

to drug sales and manufacturing. The total number of arrests for drug crimes was lower than in the early 2000s, however. In 2006, for example, there had been about 1.9 million arrests for drug-related crimes.

The total number of people incarcerated for drug crimes has also dropped slightly in recent years. According to the Department of Justice, the total prison population declined in 2012 from a peak in 2009. Fewer people were imprisoned for drug crimes, as well. From 2006 to 2011, the number of drug offenders sent to state prisons—which make up about 90 percent of the prison population—decreased by 22 percent. The percentage of prisoners in state prisons with drug offenses as the most serious offense fell from 20 percent in 2006 to 16.6 percent in 2011. In 2012, about half of all federal prisoners were nonviolent criminals with a drug offense as their most serious offense.

The statistics reflect changing state policies on drug laws. Part of the shift is due to current attitudes toward drugs, and part is a result of tough economic times after the recession of the mid-2000s. Budget constraints caused some states to reconsider whether it was worthwhile to spend a lot of money keeping people in prison for minor drug crimes. On average, it costs more than $30,000 to keep an inmate in prison for a year.

According to the Pew Research Center, forty states eased drug laws in some way between 2009 and 2013. Measures taken include decriminalization of marijuana, loosening of penalties, and amending mandatory minimum sentences. Some states have allowed more cases to be diverted from criminal courts or have sentenced certain offenders to probation rather than prison. Several states also strengthened certain drug laws during this time, or strengthened some while easing others. Arkansas, for example, added additional types of locations where selling drugs qualified for stiffer penalties, but it also reduced mandatory minimum penalties for possession and some distribution offenses.

In addition to Attorney General Holder's memo mentioned in chapter two, a new measure proposes to reduce mandatory minimum sentences for drug offenses in federal cases. This would also give judges more discretion in imposing sentences.

One of the proposed changes would address a major factor behind the racial disparities in the prison population. During the 1980s, concern over crack cocaine led to far harsher sentences for crack-cocaine offenses than powdered cocaine offenses. Since crack was used more commonly by African Americans and powdered cocaine by whites, African Americans received far longer sentences for comparable drug crimes. In 2010, Congress passed the Fair Sentencing Act, which reduced the sentencing disparity for crimes involving the two forms of the drug. Measures proposed in 2014 would make the Fair Sentencing Act retroactive, meaning that prisoners sentenced under the former guidelines could apply to have their sentences reduced.

CHAPTER 4

DRUGS AND ADOLESCENCE

D rug policies and penalties vary greatly from one state to another, and laws can vary even more for cases involving juveniles. There is no national juvenile justice system. Each state has its own set of laws and procedures for dealing with juvenile offenders. These policies can be found on state government websites. Some states have a centralized system under state control, while others are run at a local level or some combination of state and local control. The juvenile justice system even has its own terminology. Young offenders don't commit crimes; they commit "juvenile offenses." If found guilty, or "adjudicated delinquent," they don't receive a prison sentence; they're confined in "residential placement."

The juvenile justice system emphasizes rehabilitation rather than punishment to a greater extent than adult criminal courts. It functions, in some respects, as a

The most severe penalty for a young offender is residential placement. Most juvenile offenders receive a lesser sanction, such as probation.

parental stand-in. Proceedings are less formal and adversarial than criminal court trials. Judges are allowed more discretion in their rulings. Offenders are more likely to receive less restrictive penalties. Throughout the offender's involvement in the system, there are multiple points at which the offender might be diverted to a less punitive outcome than confinement.

KIDS IN THE SYSTEM

An offender's involvement in the juvenile justice system generally begins with an arrest by the police. In 2010, 1.47 million juveniles were arrested in the United States, a decrease of 21 percent from 2001. Of these, 170,600 were held for drug offenses. About 10,000 were arrested for driving under the influence and more than 88,000 for liquor law violations. Sixty-eight percent of all arrested youth were referred to juvenile court, and eight percent were referred to criminal court. The remainder was dismissed at intake by the prosecutor's office or juvenile probation department.

Nationwide, the juvenile court system handled about 1.4 million cases in 2010, including about 164,000 drug violations and 16,000 liquor law violations. The typical drug offender was older than sixteen (59 percent), male (82 percent), and white (76 percent). Likewise, the typical liquor law offender was older than sixteen (66 percent), male (68 percent), and white (89 percent).

Once an offender is referred to juvenile court, the case can be handled informally or formally. Informal handling, which is more common for less serious cases, is one means of diversion from formal juvenile court proceedings. After the case is reviewed, the offender is given a penalty, such as a referral to a social-service agency, informal probation, restitution, or a fine. The offender can generally avoid establishing a court record. In 2010, slightly less than half of all drug law violations—a little more than 80,000 cases—were handled informally, as were the majority of the liquor law violations—nearly 12,000 cases. A small number of drug cases—less than 1 percent of the total—were waived to adult criminal court.

A young offender enters a courtroom for a hearing. Cases involving serious offenses are formally adjudicated in juvenile court or transferred to adult criminal court.

In 2010, 84,000 cases involving drug violations were formally adjudicated in juvenile court—the juvenile justice system equivalent of a criminal trial—as were 4,700 liquor law violation cases. On average, offenders were adjudicated delinquent (found guilty) in about three out of five cases, including in almost 49,000 drug cases (58 percent) and 3,000 liquor law violations (63 percent). The most common penalty was probation, received by nearly 34,000 drug offenders (69 percent); 9,200 offenders (19 percent) received either "out of home placement," or imprisonment. The remaining 6,000 drug offenders (12 percent) received other penalties, such as restitution or community service. Most liquor law offenders received probation or some other lighter penalty.

One form of diversion from regular juvenile court is drug court, which may be recommended to adolescents struggling with substance abuse problems. Drug court, at times combined with mental health court, is also available in the adult system (though not yet in federal court). It operates to focus on rehabilitation, just as juvenile drug courts do. A juvenile drug court specializes in rehabilitating youth offenders. The treatment process is not like a court proceeding and resembles a collaborative effort between the offender, the offender's family, and a drug court team. A drug court judge is a key figure in the offender's recovery who often takes a much more intensive role monitoring the offender's progress than a regular court judge.

The objective of drug court is to change the offender's behavior to break the cycle of drug abuse and relapse into drug use or return to criminal activities. The process begins with screening to determine whether an offender is likely to benefit from the program—often, only nonviolent offenders are considered eligible. If the offender successfully completes treatments, the charges may be reduced or dismissed.

Evidence has shown that drug courts can help young offenders turn their lives around—at a lower cost for the state than regular juvenile court proceedings. In a study titled "The Value of Juvenile Drug Courts," researchers shared the story of "Carrie," a high school student who was struggling in school due to a problem with drugs. Carrie had completed inpatient treatment programs, but she still couldn't stay away from drugs. Her father also abused drugs, and neither of her parents was involved in helping her overcome her struggles. Carrie was accepted into a drug court program. She also moved in with an aunt who supported her progress in school and drug treatment. Carrie completed drug court and graduated from high school a straight-A student.

An adolescent doesn't have to be arrested to get into trouble for drug or alcohol use. Some schools have zero-tolerance policies for drug or alcohol use or possession. Violations can result in expulsion, suspension, or exclusion from extracurricular activities. Using drugs or alcohol at work can get an employee fired. Some employers require drug testing of workers before they can be hired and sometimes as random checks during employment.

WHAT IS HARM REDUCTION?

Drug policy in the United States focuses primarily on retribution and rehabilitation. Policy makers work to eliminate drug trafficking and abuse by punishing criminals and providing treatment programs to addicts. A third approach toward the drug problem aims to lessen the health effects of illegal drug use. The idea behind this public policy is called harm reduction.

Supporters of harm reduction efforts acknowledge that, despite the best efforts of policy makers, there always will be people using drugs and potentially damaging their own health as a side effect. Heroin users who inject the drug, for example, can contract and spread diseases such as

(continued on the next page)

Some harm-reduction programs aim to fight the spread of diseases such as HIV/AIDS. Here, a mobile van in Washington, D.C., provides clean needles to drug users.

(continued from the previous page)

hepatitis C and HIV by sharing needles with other users. One type of harm reduction effort is needle-exchange programs, in which drug users can trade their dirty needles for clean ones. Another harm reduction initiative is overdose prevention. The drug naloxone can reverse the effects of a potentially fatal overdose of heroin or other opiates. Harm reduction groups advocate making naloxone more readily available by providing the drug to police officers and emergency medical technicians or by allowing access to friends or family of drug users. Studies have shown that harm reduction programs do not lead to increases in drug use. Some cities, like New York City, have already provided the drug to paramedics, firefighters, and police officers.

Harm reduction is a controversial topic among many politicians who claim that harm reduction programs convey the message that drug use can be safe and acceptable. Federal money may not be spent on needle-exchange programs, and needle exchanges are essentially illegal in half of all states. Naloxone is available only by prescription, making it difficult to get. Nonetheless, advocates of harm reduction measures point out that heroin use has increased drastically since 2000, and that harm reduction programs could play a role in reducing the public health impact of the crisis.

TEEN TREATMENT PROGRAMS

Drug or alcohol abuse can cause an adolescent's life to spin out of control. Studies have shown that young offenders are more likely than average teens to have a substance abuse problem. Substance abuse and crime—not just offenses directly related to drugs or alcohol—tend to be linked. Drug abusers might sell drugs, they might steal to buy drugs, and they might commit crimes while under the influence of drugs. The National Institute on Drug Abuse (NIDA) recommends that all teens detained for any crime be screened for substance abuse disorders. As a juvenile court judge hands down a disposition, or court sentence, he or she might require that an offender with a substance abuse problem undergo treatment.

Treatment programs not only help offenders quit using drugs or alcohol, they reduce the chances that offenders will return to a life of crime. Such programs benefit communities and public health, as well. But only a small number of offenders are offered effective substance abuse treatment.

Court-mandated substance abuse treatment programs—which might be required of an offender as part of the sentence—begin with an assessment to decide whether a teen offender will benefit from treatment and determine what other help might be necessary. Substance abuse might occur along with other issues, such as medical problems, mental health issues, physical or emotional abuse, or trouble in school. Often, family involvement helps a young abuser through the recovery process. When family dynamics are part of the underlying problem, counseling might strengthen family functioning.

A substance abuse treatment program will likely involve the court system, substance abuse treatment providers, social service agencies, and parole or probation supervision. An offender might be monitored through drug testing during the course of the program and during probation, if required. Relapses are not uncommon, and the treatment process incorporates both rewards and punishments to motivate good behavior.

TEENS SEEKING VOLUNTARY TREATMENT

Sometimes, an adolescent doesn't need to go before a judge in court to realize that he or she needs help with a substance abuse problem. Whatever the motivation—trouble in school, a scary experience with drugs or alcohol, the urging of friends—the next step is to find substance abuse treatment resources. For many teens, confidentiality might be a concern. A teen might be nervous about seeking drug or alcohol counseling if the law requires that he or she get permission from a parent or guardian.

Federal law offers some privacy and confidentiality for teens receiving substance abuse treatment at federally funded programs and facilities. These might include hospital-based programs, private practices, or nonprofit organizations. A teen must give written consent before a treatment provider can legally disclose information to the teen's caregiver. In extraordinary circumstances—if the teen poses a threat to his or her own well-being, or to another, and lacks the capacity to consent to disclosure—caregivers may be contacted.

Most state laws do not protect teen confidentiality concerning substance abuse treatment as strictly as federal law. States may impose a minimum age for consent. Many states require parental involvement at some stage of treatment or allow doctors to notify parents without the teen's consent. Some states specifically bar teens from consenting to treatments such as methadone, which is used by recovering heroin addicts.

Juvenile drug court is a collaborative program that addresses family issues and engages parents and other caregivers in the recovery process.

The subtleties of the law are very complex, and treatment providers aren't even always certain which law applies in some circumstances. Because federal and state law might conflict, if confidentiality is a serious concern, a teen should ask the treatment provider about consent and privacy rights before applying.

Substance abuse can inflict terrible consequences, and the legal system can exact harsh penalties for drug offenses. But opportunities also exist for offenders—especially juvenile offenders—to be rehabilitated as they complete the penalty for their offense. Teens who know the law, know their rights, and recognize the consequences of their actions are well equipped for making good, responsible decisions concerning alcohol and drugs.

addiction A physical or psychological dependence on a habit-forming substance.

case A legal dispute that is heard in a court of law.

conspire To secretly plan with someone to do something that is harmful or illegal.

depressant A drug that relieves anxiety and slows physical reactions and activity.

discretion The power of a judge or other official to make judgments based on principles of law and fairness.

disposition A final arrangement; settlement.

diversion A type of informal probation that proposes alternatives to conviction, used in both juvenile and adult court.

felony A serious crime punishable in state or federal court by more than a year imprisonment and, in some circumstances, by death.

hallucinogen One of a diverse group of drugs that alters perceptions, thoughts, and emotions.

juvenile A minor who has committed a crime.

misdemeanor A minor crime; specifically, one punishable by a fine and/or by a term of imprisonment less than one year.

narcotic A drug that induces numbness or stupor.

offender One who has committed an illegal act.

opiate A drug that contains opium or opium derivatives.

opioid A synthetic compound that possesses some properties characteristic of opiates.

paraphernalia Implements used for preparing or taking drugs.

penalty A punishment imposed for breaking a rule or law.

probation The act of suspending an offender's sentence and allowing him or her to go free subject to certain conditions.

status offense Conduct that is illegal for a minor but noncriminal for an adult.

stimulant A class of drug that elevates mood and increases energy and alertness.

traffic To engage in illegal or improper commercial activity.

American Civil Liberties Union (ACLU)
125 Broad Street, 18th Floor
New York, NY 10004
(212) 549-2500
Web site: http://www.aclu.org
The ACLU works to protect liberty and defends individual
    rights and liberties that the Constitution and laws of
    the United States guarantee everyone in the nation.

Canadian Centre on Drug Abuse
75 Albert Street, Suite 500
Ottawa, ON K1P 5E7
Canada
(613) 235-4048
Website: http://www.ccsa.ca
The Centre on Drug Abuse works to reduce alcohol- and
    drug-related harm.

Drug Enforcement Administration (DEA)
Attn: Office of Diversion Control
8701 Morrissette Drive
Springfield, VA 22152
(202) 307-1000
Website: http://www.justice.gov/dea/index.shtml
The DEA is the official Department of Justice agency
    charged with enforcing controlled substance laws
    and regulations.

Drug Policy Alliance
131 West 33rd Street, 15th Floor
New York, NY 10001

(212) 613-8020
Website: http://www.drugpolicy.org
The Drug Policy Alliance aims to advance policies and attitudes that best reduce the harms of both drug use and drug prohibition.

Food and Drug Administration (FDA)
10903 New Hampshire Avenue
Silver Spring, MD 20993-0002
(888) 463-6332
Website: http://www.fda.gov
The FDA is responsible for protecting public health by assuring the safety and security of the nation's food supply and human and veterinary drugs.

National Anti-Drug Strategy
Website: http://www.nationalantidrugstrategy.gc.ca
Canada's National Anti-Drug Strategy works for the prevention and treatment of drug abuse and enforcement of drug laws.

National Center for Juvenile Justice (NCJJ)
3700 South Water Street, Suite 200
Pittsburgh, PA 15203
(412) 227-6950
Website: http://www.ncjj.org
A division of the National Council of Juvenile and Family Court Judges, NCJJ aims to provide effective justice for children and their families through research and technical assistance.

Office of Juvenile Justice and Delinquency Prevention (OJJDP)
810 Seventh Street NW
Washington, DC 20531
(202) 307–5911
Website: http://www.ojjdp.gov
Part of the U.S. Department of Justice, OJJDP provides national leadership, coordination, and resources to prevent and respond to juvenile delinquency and victimization.

Substance Abuse and Mental Health Services Administration (SAMHSA)
1 Choke Cherry Road
Rockville, MD 20857
(877) 726-4727
Website: http://www.samhsa.gov
SAMHSA aims to reduce the impact of substance abuse and mental illness on America's communities.

WEBSITES

Because of the changing nature of Internet links, Rosen Publishing has developed an online list of websites related to the subject of this book. This site is updated regularly. Please use this link to access this list:

http://www.rosenlinks.com/KYR/Alco

FOR FURTHER READING

Adamec, Christine. *Amphetamines and Methamphetamine*. New York, NY: Chelsea House Publishers, 2011.

Adamec, Christine. *Barbiturates and Other Depressants*. New York, NY: Chelsea House Publishers, 2011.

Espejo, Roman, ed. *Club Drugs*. Detroit, MI: Greenhaven Press, 2009.

Gass, Justin T. *Alcohol*. New York, NY: Chelsea House Publishers, 2010.

Hecht, Alan. *Antidepressants and Antianxiety Drugs*. New York, NY: Chelsea House Publishers, 2010.

Hecht, Alan. *Cocaine and Crack*. New York, NY: Chelsea House Publishers, 2011.

Hofmann, Albert. *LSD: My Problem Child*. New York, NY: Oxford University Press, 2013.

Kane, Brigid M. *Marijuana*. New York, NY: Chelsea House Publishers, 2011.

Kramer, Ann. *Teen FAQ: Drugs*. Mankato, MN: Franklin Watts, 2010.

Kuhar, Michael. *The Addicted Brain: Why We Abuse Drugs, Alcohol, and Nicotine*. Upper Saddle River, NJ: FT Press, 2011.

Magill, Elizabeth, ed. *Drug Information for Teens*, 3rd ed. Detroit, MI: Omnigraphics, 2011.

May, Suellen. *Ritalin and Related Drugs*. New York, NY: Chelsea House Publishers, 2010.

Nelson, David. *Teen Drug Abuse*. Detroit, MI: Greenhaven Press, 2010.

Olive, M. Foster. *Ecstasy*. New York, NY: Chelsea House Publishers, 2010.

Rodger, Marguerite. *Party and Club Drugs*. New York, NY: Crabtree Publishing, 2012.

Rooney, Anne. *Dealing with Drugs*. Mankato, MN: Amicus, 2011.

Sadler, Katharine. *What Adults Need to Know About Kids and Substance Use: Dealing with Alcohol, Tobacco, and Other Drugs*. Minneapolis, MN: Search Institute Press, 2011.

Shannon, Joyce Brennfleck. *Drug Abuse Sourcebook*, 3rd ed. Detroit, MI: Omnigraphics, 2010.

Sheff, David. *Clean: Overcoming Addiction and Ending America's Greatest Tragedy*. Boston, MA: Houghton Mifflin Harcourt, 2013.

Sheff, Nic. *We All Fall Down: Living with Addiction*. New York, NY: Little, Brown, 2011.

Shooter, Debbie and William Shooter. *Drugs and Alcohol 101*. Orlando, FL: Off Campus Education and Publishing Inc., 2010.

Williams, Heidi. *Juvenile Crime: Issues that Concern You*. San Diego, CA: Greenhaven Press, 2010.

BIBLIOGRAPHY

American Civil Liberties Union. "The War on Marijuana in Black and White." June 2013. Retrieved May 18, 2014 (http://www.aclu.org).

Barcott, Bruce. "The Great Marijuana Experiment: A Tale of Two Drug Wars." *Rolling Stone*, January 3, 2014. Retrieved March 7, 2014. (http://www.rollingstone.com).

Carson, E. Ann, and Daniela Golinelli. "U.S. Prisoners in 2012: Trends in Admissions and Releases, 1991–2012." U.S Department of Justice Bureau of Justice Statistics, December 2013. Retrieved May 18, 2014 (http://www.bjs.gov).

Centers for Disease Control and Prevention. "Fact Sheets—Age 21 Minimum Legal Drinking Age." March 14, 2014. Retrieved May 18, 2014 (http://www.cdc.gov/alcohol/fact-sheets/mlda.htm).

Centers for Disease Control and Prevention. "Policy Impact: Prescription Painkiller Overdoses." Revised July 2, 2013. Retrieved May 18, 2014 (http://www.cdc.gov).

Centers for Disease Control and Prevention. "Teen Drinking and Driving, a Dangerous Mix." October 2012. Retrieved May 18, 2014 (http://www.cdc.gov).

Cicero, Theodore J., Matthew S. Ellis, Hilary L. Surratt, and Steven P. Kurtz. "The Changing Face of Heroin Use in the United States." *JAMA Psychiatry*, May 28, 2014.

Cole, James M. "Memorandum for All United States Attorneys: Guidance Regarding Marijuana Enforcement." U.S. Department of Justice, Office of the Deputy Attorney General, August 29, 2013. Retrieved May 18, 2014 (http://www.justice.gov).

DeSilver, Drew. "Feds May Be Rethinking the Drug War, but States Have Been Leading the Way." Pew Research Center, April 2, 2014. Retrieved May 18, 2014 (http://www.pewresearch.org).

Fabricant, M. Chris. *Busted! Drug War Survival Skills: From the Buy to the Bust to Begging for Mercy*. New York, NY: HarperCollins, 2005.

FBI Criminal Justice Information Services Division. "Crime in the United States, 2012." 2013. Retrieved May 18, 2014 (http://www.fbi.gov).

Flatow, Nicole. "Juvenile Arrests Drop 20 Percent in California After Marijuana Decriminalization Law." ThinkProgress, November 27, 2012. Retrieved May 18, 2014 (http://thinkprogress.org).

Frosch, Dan. "Measures to Legalize Marijuana Are Passed." *New York Times*, November 6, 2013.

Gahlinger, Paul. *Illegal Drugs: A Complete Guide to Their History, Chemistry, Use, and Abuse*. New York, NY: Plume, 2004.

Goldstein, Margaret J. *Legalizing Drugs: Crime Stopper or Social Risk?* Minneapolis, MN: Twenty-First Century Books, 2010.

Goodman, J. David. "In Effort to Fight Overdoses, Staten Island Officers Will Soon Carry Heroin Antidote." *New York Times*, April 17, 2014.

Jacobs, Tom. *What Are My Rights? Q&A About Teens and the Law*, 3rd ed. Minneapolis, MN: Free Spirit Publishing, 2011.

Knefel, John. "The Controversial Answer to America's Heroin Surge." BuzzFeed, May 15, 2014. Retrieved May 18, 2014 (http://www.buzzfeed.com/johnknefel/the-controversial-answer-to-americas-heroin-surge).

Kuhn, Cynthia, et al. *Buzzed: The Straight Facts About the Most Used and Abused Drugs from Alcohol to Ecstasy.* New York, NY: W. W. Norton & Company, 2008.

Kuhn, Cynthia, et al. *Just Say Know: Talking with Kids About Drugs and Alcohol.* New York, NY: W. W. Norton & Company, 2002.

Lu, Yi. "Medical Marijuana Policy in the United States." HOPES, May 15, 2012. Retrieved May 18, 2014 (http://web.stanford.edu).

Motel, Seth. "6 Facts About Marijuana." Pew Research Center, April 7, 2014. Retrieved May 18, 2014 (http://www.pewresearch.org).

Nagourney, Adam, and Rick Lyman. "Few Problems with Cannabis for California." *New York Times*, October 27, 2013.

National Institute on Alcohol Abuse and Alcoholism. "Alcohol Policy Information System." Retrieved May 18, 2014 (https://alcoholpolicy.niaaa.nih.gov/Home.html).

National Institute on Drug Abuse. "DrugFacts: High-School and Youth Trends." January 2014. Retrieved May 18, 2014 (http://www.drugabuse.gov).

National Institute on Drug Abuse. "DrugFacts: Nationwide Trends." Revised January 2014. Retrieved May 18, 2014 (http://www.drugabuse.gov).

Okrent, Daniel. *Last Call: The Rise and Fall of Prohibition.* New York, NY: Scribner, 2011.

Pew Research Center for the People and the Press. "America's New Drug Policy Landscape: Two-Thirds

Favor Treatment, Not Jail, for Use of Heroin, Cocaine."
April 2, 2014. Retrieved May 18, 2014 (http://www
.people-press.org).

Puzzanchera, Charles. "Juvenile Arrests 2010." Pittsburgh,
PA: National Center for Juvenile Justice, December
2013. Retrieved May 18, 2014 (http://www.ojjdp.gov/
pubs/242770.pdf).

Puzzanchera, Charles, and Sarah Hockenberry. "Juvenile
Court Statistics 2010: Report." Pittsburgh, PA:
National Center for Juvenile Justice, June 2013.
Retrieved May 18, 2014 (http://www.ncjj.org/pdf/
jcsreports/jcs2010.pdf).

Puzzanchera, Charles, and Crystal Robson. "Delinquency
Cases in Juvenile Court, 2010." Pittsburgh, PA:
National Center for Juvenile Justice, February 2014.
Retrieved May 18, 2014 (http://www.ojjdp.gov/
pubs/243041.pdf).

Rand, Michael R., et al. "Alcohol and Crime: Data from 2002
to 2008." Bureau of Justice Statistics, September 3,
2010. Retrieved May 18, 2014 (http://www.bjs.gov).

Remnick, David. "Going the Distance: On and Off the Road
with Barack Obama." *New Yorker*, January 27, 2014.
Retrieved May 18, 2014 (http://www.newyorker
.com).

Simkins, Sandra. *When Kids Get Arrested: What Every Adult
Should Know.* New Brunswick, NJ: Rutgers University
Press, 2009.

Truly, Traci. *Teen Rights (And Responsibilities): A Legal Guide
for Teens and the Adults in Their Lives,* 2nd ed.
Naperville, IL: Sphinx Publishing, 2005.

U.S. Department of Justice Drug Enforcement Agency. "Federal Trafficking Penalties." Retrieved May 18, 2014 (http://www.justice.gov).

U.S. Department of Justice Drug Enforcement Agency. "National Drug Threat Assessment Summary 2013." November 2013. Retrieved May 18, 2014 (http://www.justice.gov).

Van Wormer, Jacqueline, and Faith Lutze. "Exploring the Evidence: The Value of Juvenile Drug Courts." Juvenile and Family Justice Today, Summer 2011. Retrieved May 22, 2014 (http://www.courtswv.gov).

White House, Office of National Drug Control Policy. "Marijuana Resource Center." Retrieved May 18, 2014 (http://www.whitehouse.gov/ondcp/marijuanainfo).

White House, Office of National Drug Control Policy. "Prescription Drug Abuse." Retrieved May 18, 2014 (http://www.whitehouse.gov/ondcp/prescription -drug-abuse).

INDEX

A

alcohol, 7–16
    crime and, 10–11
    driving and, 11–12
    legal drinking age, 8–10
    Prohibition, 14–15
    as public health problem, 7, 14
    underage drinking,
        8, 9–10, 11–12, 13,
        16, 41, 42, 43
American Civil Liberties Union
    (ACLU), 4–5, 28

C

Coffey, John, Jr., 29–30
Comprehensive Drug Abuse
    Prevention and Control Act,
    18, 31, 35
Controlled Substances Act, 18, 24

D

depressants, 31
drug court, 43–44
Drug Enforcement Agency (DEA),
    33, 35, 36
drugs, illegal and illicit, 29–39
    crime and, 30, 35, 38–39,
        46–47
    marijuana, 4–5, 17–28, 35
    minors and, 40–49
    penalties for dealing and
      trafficking, 33, 34, 39

    penalties for possession of,
        33–34, 39
    as public health problem, 30, 35
drunk driving, 11–12

H

hallucinogens, 31
    research into treating mental
        illness, 24
harm-reduction efforts, 45–46
heroin, 29–30, 36, 37,
    45–46, 48
Holder, Eric, 20, 39

L

lawyer, consulting a, 12, 13

M

marijuana, 17–28, 36
    arrests for, 4–5, 35
    crime and, 26–28
    decriminalization of, 27, 30
    federal guidelines concerning,
      20–21
    history of 17–18
    legalization of, 17, 21–22, 23,
      24–26, 30
    medical use of, 18–19,
      21–23, 26
    minors and, 18, 20, 26, 27, 28
    penalties for growing and
      selling, 19–20, 28

ABOUT THE AUTHOR

Corona Brezina has written more than a dozen young adult books, including several focused on health and legal issues concerning teens, such as *The Truth About LSD and Hallucinogens* and *FAQ Teen Life: Frequently Asked Questions About Juvenile Detention*. She lives in Chicago.

ABOUT THE EXPERT REVIEWER

Lindsay A. Lewis, Esq., is a practicing criminal defense attorney in New York City, where she handles a wide range of matters, from those discussed in this series to high-profile federal criminal cases. She believes that each and every defendant deserves a vigorous and informed defense. Ms. Lewis is a graduate of the Benjamin N. Cardozo School of Law and Vassar College.

PHOTO CREDITS